JUL - - 2016

Get to Know

Mary
Cassatt

Charlotte Taylor

Enslow Publishing
101 W. 23rd Street
Suite 240
New York, NY 10011
USA
enslow.com

Published in 2016 by Enslow Publishing, LLC
101 W. 23rd Street, Suite 240, New York, NY 10011

Library of Congress Cataloging-in-Publication Data

Taylor, Charlotte, 1978– author.
 Get to know Mary Cassatt / Charlotte Taylor.
     pages cm. — (Famous artists)
 Includes bibliographical references and index.
 Summary: "Describes the life and work of painter Mary Cassatt"— Provided by publisher.
 ISBN 978-0-7660-7234-3 (library binding)
 ISBN 978-0-7660-7232-9 (pbk)
 ISBN 978-0-7660-7233-6 (6pk)
 1. Cassatt, Mary, 1844-1926—Juvenile literature. 2. Painters—United Statees—Biography—Juvenile
literature. I. Title.
 ND237.C3T39 2016
 759.13—dc23
 [B]
                                    2015029901

Printed in the United States of America

To Our Readers: We have done our best to make sure all website addresses in this book were active
and appropriate when we went to press. However, the author and the publisher have no control over and
assume no liability for the material available on those websites or any websites they may link to. Any
comments or suggestions can be sent by e-mail to customerservice@enslow.com.

Portions of this book originally appeared in *Mary Cassatt The Life of an Artist* by Carolyn Casey.

Photo Credits: Cover, p. 1 © Everett Collection Historical / Alamy; throughout book Rudchenko Liliia/
Shutterstock.com (painting background), Mostovyi Sergii Igorevich/Shutterstock.com (palate and
brushes dingbat), foxie/Shutterstock.com (brushstrokes), rzstudio/Shutterstock.com (paint brush); p. 4
© Folio / Alamy Stock Photo; p. 6 Mother and Child, 1897 (pastel on paper), Cassatt, Mary Stevenson
(1844–1926) / Musee d'Orsay, Paris, France / Bridgeman Images; p. 9 Kean Collection/Archive Photos/
Getty Images; p. 10 Time Life Pictures/The LIFE Pictures Collection/Getty Images; p. 11 Smithsonian
American Art Museum, Washington, DC / Art Resource, NY; p. 12 Madame de Senonnes, 1814-16
(oil on canvas), Ingres, Jean Auguste Dominique (1780-1867) / Musee des Beaux-Arts, Nantes, France
/ Bridgeman Images; p. 14 Curt Teich Postcard Archives/Archive Photos/Getty Images; p. 15 Visions
of America/Universal Images Group/Getty Images; p.16 Science & Society Picture Library/SSPL/Getty
Images; p. 17 Antoinette at her dresser, Cassatt, Mary Stevenson (1844–1926) / Collection of Mrs.
Samuel E. Johnson, Chicago, IL, USA / Bridgeman Images; p. 19 Mondadori Portfolio/Hulton Fine Art
Collection/Getty Images; p. 20 Heritage Images/Hulton Fine Art Collection/Getty Images; p. 22 Universal
History Archive/ Universal Images Group/Getty Images; p. 24 Two Seated Women (oil on canvas),
Cassatt, Mary Stevenson (1844–1926) / Private Collection / Bridgeman Images; p. 26 National Portrait
Gallery, Smithsonian Institution/Art Resource, NY; p. 28 DEA/G. DAGLI ORTI/ De Agostini/Getty
Images; p. 30 Spanish Dancer, Cassatt, Mary Stevenson (1844–1926) / Private Collection / Bridgeman
Images; p. 32 The New York Public Library/Art Resource/NY; p. 34 © PAINTING / Alamy Stock Photo;
p. 36 Culture Club/Hulton Archive/Getty Images; p.39 Heritage images/Hulton Fine Art Collection/Getty
Images; p. 40 © Niday Picture Library / Alamy Stock Photo; p. 43 GraphicaArtis/Archive Photos/Getty
Images; p. 44 © Sergey Komarov-Kohl / Alamy Stock Photo.

Contents

Chapter 1

Breaking the Rules

Mary Cassatt was born over a hundred and fifty years ago. At that time, most girls dreamed of getting married and having children. Very few women had jobs, and almost none were professional artists.

Mary Cassatt was different. As a teenager, she decided she wanted to become a painter. She later traveled by herself all over Europe at a time when it was rare for a woman to do so. And unlike most women of that time, she never married.

A New Movement

From the beginning, Cassatt was determined to become famous and to paint in her own style. Rather than staying with the painting styles everyone else used, she insisted on breaking the rules. Cassatt was the only American member of the French Impressionist movement, a group of artists working in the late

Little Anne Sucking Her Finger, Embraced by Her Mother (1897, Musée d'Orsay, Paris). Cassatt captured the secure feeling of a child in its mother's arms. Look at how the mother completely encircles the child's body.

nineteenth century. The Impressionists changed the entire world of the visual arts.

Cassatt became one of the most famous women painters in history. Her paintings and pastel drawings are recognized around the world for their style. Cassatt seemed to step into the private lives of the people she painted.

But Cassatt's success came slowly, and it was a struggle. She had to convince even her own family to help her become a painter.

Chapter 2

Early Days in Europe

Mary Stevenson Cassatt was born into a large, well-to-do family on May 22, 1844. They lived in Allegheny City, Pennsylvania. Young Mary had one older sister, two older brothers, and one younger brother.

Mary's family lived well. They had more money than most American families at that time. Mary's father, Robert Simpson Cassatt, was a successful businessman. He and Katherine Johnston Cassatt, Mary's mother, liked going to parties and enjoyed the arts.

When Mary was seven, her parents decided to move the family to Europe. They felt their children would get a better education there than in America. They sailed across the Atlantic Ocean and made their new home in Paris, France.

Two years later, the Cassatts moved to Germany. Sadly, while they were living there, Mary's older brother Robbie died of a bone disease in his knee that he had had for several years.

Cassatt's birthplace, Allegheny City, Pennsylvania, is now part of the city of Pittsburgh. The illustration shows the Union Malleable iron works, which would have been in full production when Casatt was a child.

The grieving Cassatt family decided to move back to the United States. One son, Alexander, stayed behind to study in Germany.

Inspired by Art

Right before they left Europe, Mary and her family visited the Louvre, a museum that held the best art collection in Paris. She saw many great paintings and sculptures. The Cassatts also visited the World's Fair in Paris. Mary was amazed by some of the art she saw there.

This illustration shows the Louvre Museum in Paris, France, in the 1850s.

Mary was just eleven years old when she announced that she was going to be an artist. Since there were very few female artists when Mary was a girl, this was a startling thing for her parents to hear.

In 1855, Mary's family returned to Philadelphia. Mary studied French, a language she would later speak all the time as an artist in Paris. Mary also began learning how to be a fine horseback rider. Riding horses was something she loved for the rest of her life.

Sara in a Green Bonnet (1901, National Gallery of Art, Washington, DC). Cassatt captured little Sara's sweet hint of a smile.

Cassatt was greatly influenced by the works of artists she saw at the Louvre in Paris. One of these artists was Jean-Auguste-Dominique Ingres, a French painter. Ingres painted this portrait, *Madame de Sennones*, in 1814. Much of Cassatt's art showed the same relaxed pose and natural expression.

Chapter 3

Art Student

Cassatt's parents were not happy when she decided to become an artist. But they still helped her by paying for art classes for many years. When Cassatt was fifteen, she stopped going to her regular school. She wanted to study only art.

The next year, Cassatt convinced her parents to let her take a drawing class at the Pennsylvania Academy of the Fine Arts in Philadelphia. This art school was one of the few that allowed women to enroll. Cassatt and her best friend, Eliza Haldeman, took classes together. They visited art collections to study the styles of famous artists.

It is common for art students to learn to paint by making copies of famous paintings. Even as a student, Cassatt preferred to copy paintings of ordinary people rather than formal portraits of wealthy people.

Cassatt first learned about art at the Academy of Fine Arts in Philadelphia, Pennsylvania, seen here.

As a teenager, Cassatt complained about women not being allowed to do the same things men did. But she did not let that stop her. She was determined to be a successful artist.

Off to Paris

She stayed at the academy for four years and became very skilled as a painter. But Cassatt knew she needed to study in Paris to be successful. That was where many of the great artists lived and worked.

Art students often learn to paint by copying paintings by master artists. At museums such as the Louvre in Paris, the Metropolitan Museum of Art in New York City, and the Philadelphia Museum of Art, you can often see art students practicing at their easels.

Cassatt's father was upset when she told the family she wanted to go to France. However, when she was twenty-one, he agreed to let her go and gave her money for the trip. Her mother traveled with her to Paris. Her friend Eliza joined her there a few months later.

Most art schools in Paris did not allow women to enroll. Those that did offered very few classes for them. But Cassatt did not give up. She and Eliza took private classes from successful painters. They went to museums to copy the works of master artists.

The famous Louvre museum became their school. Most women artists in those days did not do original work but instead sold the copies they made of famous paintings. But Cassatt made it clear to her friends that she wanted to create her own paintings.

This photograph shows Paris around the time when Cassatt moved there. The Louvre is in the center.

Antoinette at her Dresser (1909, Private Collection). A woman looks at herself in a mirror with another mirror behind her, reflecting the back of her head. Viewers see Antoinette's face and reflection, but not the same view she sees of herself.

Chapter 4

Painting Ordinary People

After spending a couple of years studying art in Paris, Cassatt decided it was time for a change. She and her friend Eliza moved to the French countryside. They began painting villagers living their everyday lives.

Most artists in those days painted formal portraits of wealthy people. Families would dress in their finest clothes and stand stiffly for hours in their fanciest room while an artist painted them.

Mary Cassatt discovered that she preferred painting simple farmers and their families going about their lives, raising their children, and doing ordinary things.

First she would make a quick sketch. Then she would turn the sketches into beautiful paintings. She captured images such as a mother giving her baby a bath, a farmer taking care of his animals, or people laughing together in a restaurant.

Young Woman Sewing in the Garden (1880–1882, Musée d'Orsay, Paris). Sewing was a common activity for young women in the nineteenth century.

Maternal Kiss (1896, Philadelphia Museum of Art). In this painting, Cassatt places the faces of mother and child so close that they almost appear as one.

Her paintings showed movement and life. She used paint to show the natural light. Just as she had hoped, her own personal style began to develop. Some of her Paris teachers liked these unusual paintings.

The Salon

At that time there was an important art show held in Paris every year. It was called the Paris Salon Art Exhibition, or "the Salon"

Art Smarts

Mary Cassatt was famous for her pictures of women with children. She often showed them doing ordinary things, such as bathing, getting dressed, or reading a book together. In some paintings, she showed the two simply sitting together, almost always tenderly touching. Her subjects almost always look fully relaxed in their closeness.

Summertime (1894, Armand Hammer Museum of Art and Cultural Center, Los Angeles, CA). Like many of Cassatt's paintings of the time, this work depicts a scene from the country life of everyday people.

for short. Many artists dedicated their entire year to making something the Salon judges would include in the show.

Cassatt's teachers chose one of her paintings for the Salon, and it was accepted. It was a picture of a peasant girl playing a mandolin.

This was the first time one of Cassatt's paintings had been selected for any contest. It was unusual for the Salon judges to choose a young woman's work. It was even more unusual for them to select a work of art by an American artist.

Some people liked Cassatt's paintings from the French countryside. But the people who judged the show said they were too informal. They said the unusual style showed Cassatt's lack of experience.

Two Women Seated by a Woodland Stream (1869, Private Collection). This country scene is one of Cassatt's early works.

Chapter 5

The Artist at Work

In 1870, war broke out between France and Germany. It was no longer safe to live in Paris. Cassatt and many other Americans were forced to return to the United States.

Cassatt set up a studio in Philadelphia. She was joined there by some other American artists who had fled Europe. However, her art was unknown in America and did not sell well.

She missed the experience of being surrounded by art and artists in Europe. She tried showing some of her paintings at an art store in Chicago. But a few days after she took them there, they were burned in the Great Chicago Fire of 1871.

A Job in Italy

Also in that same year, the Catholic bishop in Pittsburgh offered Cassatt three hundred dollars to create some paintings for him. The project would involve her traveling to Parma, Italy, to paint copies of two famous religious paintings for the

Self-Portrait (around 1880, National Gallery of Art, Washington, DC). Cassatt's watercolor painting of herself is not detailed and realistic. Rather, it just gives us an idea, or impression, of the subject.

new Saint Paul's Cathedral in Pittsburgh. This would be her first paying job as an artist.

Cassatt was eager to return to Europe. She packed her supplies and boarded a ship with her close friend, artist Emily Sartain.

The work she was copying was by an artist named Correggio. He was one of Italy's most famous painters. He had lived more than three hundred years before Cassatt was born.

In Italy, besides making the copies for the cathedral, Cassatt also created other paintings. These got a lot of attention. Her friend Emily said that everyone in Parma was talking about Cassatt's work.

One of these paintings showed people at a huge carnival. Another showed a woman following a god from Roman mythology. Cassatt blended her own ideas with what she learned from copying other artists.

Finding Her Style

Art critics in Italy and France praised Cassatt's ability to do a formal religious painting as well as a lively carnival image. An American collector bought her *During Carnival* painting for $200. This was the first time Cassatt was paid for truly original work.

Madonna Adoring the Christ Child (1524–1526) is a well-known Correggio painting. The artist's real name was Antonio Allegri, and this painting now hangs in the Uffizi Gallery in his hometown of Florence, Italy.

Later, she traveled from Italy to Spain. This time she traveled alone. In Spain, Cassatt painted bullfights as well as scenes from the lives of ordinary Spanish people. She also studied the works of Spanish artists, such as Velásquez and Murillo. She loved the experience. As she wrote to a friend, "I really feel as if it was intended I should be a Spaniard and quite a mistake I was born in America."

Cassatt wanted to make sure her work became known in the United States as well as in Europe. She sent her collection of Spanish paintings back to America to be shown in an exhibit.

Spanish Dancer Wearing a Lace Mantilla (1873, Private Collection). Cassatt painted this during her trip through Spain.

Chapter 6

Cassatt and the Impressionists

Four years after leaving the country, Cassatt finally returned to France. Her older sister, Lydia, moved to Paris with her. The two women often went to the theater and opera. Mary created many paintings of women in the audience watching the shows. Her paintings showed emotion and energy. She earned money by painting portraits for wealthy tourists.

For months, Cassatt worked hard on two portraits she hoped would be chosen for the Salon. But the Salon judges would include only images that lived up to their rigid standards. Cassatt was very disappointed that only one of her paintings was accepted.

Some art critics liked her style, but others did not. Cassatt felt frustrated. It seemed to her that so many critics did not want artists to try anything new, such as painting ordinary people doing ordinary things.

Woman Seated in a Loge (around 1881, New York Public Library). The subject of this painting is a woman at the theater who is looking at the stage through binoculars. Attending the theater was a common activity for wealthy people in Paris, including Cassatt.

A New Friend

One day, Cassatt saw a drawing by someone named Edgar Degas displayed in a shop window. She loved the drawing and kept returning to study Degas's style.

Before long, Cassatt and Degas met. This began a friendship that lasted a lifetime. They did a great deal to help each other's careers. Late in her life, Cassatt described Degas as "the most important artist in my life."

Degas told her about a group of twenty-six painters he had joined who were experimenting with new painting styles. At that

Art Smarts

After she met Degas, Cassatt began using pastels in her work. Many people believe that "pastel" means a pale color. In art, a pastel is a powdered substance that is ground into a paste. It is then rolled into a stick. Pastels do not contain any oils, so they are very pure and permanent. Pastel colors can be any shade from soft to very bold.

Cassatt's close friend Edgar Degas painted her in the 1880s. *Mary Cassatt* hangs in the National Gallery of Art in Washington, DC.

time these painters called themselves the Independents. They later came to be known as the Impressionists.

A Different Kind of Art

The Impressionists used quick brush strokes and light, bright colors. They often worked outdoors in the natural light of the sun. They wanted their art to have a spontaneous, on-the-spot feeling. They wanted to capture an impression of what they saw, with all the light and color of that exact moment.

Older, more traditional paintings had a darker look. They were more detailed and looked realistic—almost like photographs. They took much longer to make.

The new group of artists began putting on their own art shows. These shows got a lot of attention. Finally, Impressionist art was being noticed.

Degas invited Cassatt to join the new group.

"I accepted with joy," she wrote. "I hated conventional art. I began to live."

In 1879, when Cassatt was thirty-four, the Impressionists had their fourth art show. She showed eleven of her paintings in it. About sixteen thousand visitors came to see the show.

Cassatt became famous after so many people saw her work. Her colors were considered very bold. Some critics liked her strong colors, but others did not.

Boulevard Montmarte in Paris was a popular gathering place for Impressionists in the 1870s and 1880s. Cassatt's studio was located there.

Chapter 7

Success at Last

By 1880, Cassatt had a successful career as an artist. She had made twenty-nine paintings, and her work was selling well.

At about this time, Cassatt's parents moved in with her and Lydia in Paris. Lydia had been diagnosed with a deadly kidney disease. Their parents moved to Paris to help run the household so that Cassatt could have time to paint.

She now spent a lot of time at home. Her parents often modeled for her. She was able to create portraits of their daily life that were touching, funny, and even sad.

Lydia died in 1881. Mary was so overcome with sadness that she stopped painting for six months.

When she returned to her work, Cassatt did many paintings of mothers and their children. These were to become her most famous images.

Cassatt was a good friend to many artists. When she was in her forties, she helped other European artists by encouraging

Mother and Child (1890, Pushkin Museum of Fine Art, Moscow, Russia). After Cassatt's sister died, she painted many mothers and children.

American collectors and museums to buy their work. People valued her opinion of other people's work.

Japanese Art

In 1890, Cassatt saw an exhibit of Japanese woodblock prints at the École des Beaux-Arts (School of Fine Arts) in Paris. These prints featured simple scenes of everyday life in Japan using bright, bold colors. During this time, many French artists became interested in making prints in Japan's simple, clean style of art.

Cassatt decided to make prints. But rather than making prints of Japanese images as some French artists did, Cassatt chose to make prints of European women working in their homes. Her works are considered some of the most valuable prints made during that time.

In 1893, Cassatt had her first large solo show in Paris. She included about a hundred of her paintings, prints, and pastels. The show was a great success. Even the critics praised her work.

The Mural Project

That same year, some Americans chose Cassatt to paint a huge mural for the 1893 Chicago World's Fair. Her mural would take up one entire wall of the Women's Building.

The Fitting (1891, Private Collection). This work combined both Japanese and Impressionist styles to create something totally unique.

Art Smarts

Cassatt was inspired by Japanese woodblock prints. They are made by carving a picture into a wood block, then putting paint or ink on the block and pressing the block onto paper to create an image. The same block can be used again and again.

The mural was fourteen feet tall and fifty-eight feet wide. In order to work on a mural so large, Cassatt turned a large greenhouse in Bachivillers, France, into a studio. She set up pulleys to raise and lower the mural while she worked on it.

This was an important time for women in Europe and the United States. Many people were fighting for women to be given the right to vote in elections. The Women's Building at the Chicago World's Fair was an important place to show off the talents of women. One wall would show women from the past, while Cassatt's mural would show modern women.

Cassatt's mural had three separate frames. The first featured young girls in the quest for fame. In the second, young women plucked the fruits of knowledge. In the third, women created art, music, and dance.

Many people did not like Cassatt's mural. The details were hard to see from the ground. The light colors she used did not work well on a mural. But even though the mural was considered a failure, Mary Cassatt's name finally became known in the United States. In 1895, she had a major show in New York that included many mother and child paintings. Art critics in New York admired her work.

Final Years

In her sixties, Cassatt began to have health problems. It was hard for her to paint. She became more and more active in women's issues. In the early 1900s, she worked hard to help convince the US government to allow women to vote.

Cassatt had many artist friends, but she also missed her family. By now, both of her parents had died. In addition, Cassatt had problems in both eyes and was losing her sight. She had surgery four times but nothing helped. She became nearly blind.

When she was seventy, Cassatt had to stop painting. During the remaining twelve years of her life, she often felt sad and frustrated. Some people said she had a bad temper.

Nevertheless, Cassatt continued to show and sell her earlier work. In 1904 France awarded Cassatt the Legion of Honor for

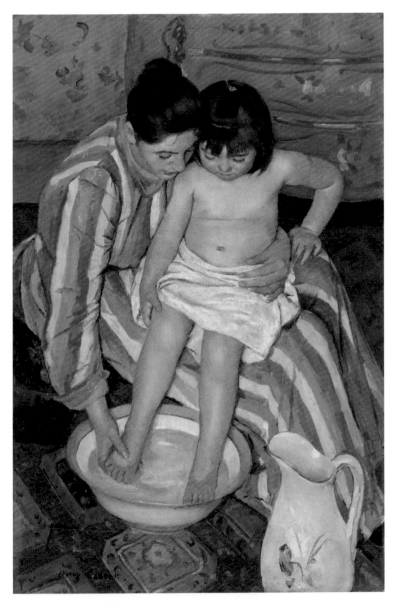

The Child's Bath (1893, Art Institute of Chicago). This is one of Cassatt's best-known paintings.

her work as a painter. It was rare for a woman, and especially an American, to get such an award. In 1914 the Pennsylvania Academy of the Fine Arts—Cassatt's first art school—awarded her the Gold Medal of Honor.

Cassatt died in France on June 14, 1926, when she was eighty-two years old.

Today, Cassatt's paintings are in many museums. Her work is included in most exhibits of Impressionist art. The US Postal Service issued stamps in 2003 honoring four of her paintings. People still enjoy looking at her work.

Throughout her life, Mary Cassatt followed her own dreams. She challenged people's views of what women could accomplish and ignored those who tried to discourage her.

Long after her death, Mary Cassatt continues to inspire artists and art lovers all over the world.

Timeline

1844—Born Mary Stevenson Cassatt on May 22 in Allegheny City, Pennsylvania.

1851—Family moves to Europe for four years.

1865—Moves on her own to Paris to study art.

1868—Is honored by having one of her paintings selected for the Paris Salon art exhibit.

1870—Returns to Philadelphia.

1871—Travels to Parma, Italy, to make copies of Correggio paintings.

1874—Settles in Paris with her sister, Lydia.

1879—Exhibits art in the Impressionists' show.

1890—Begins creating Japanese-style prints.

1893—Has first large solo show in Paris. Paints mural for Chicago World's Fair.

1904—Awarded France's Legion of Honor.

1926—Dies in France on June 14 at age eighty-two.

2003—US Postal Service issues set of stamps showing four Cassatt paintings.

2014—National Gallery of Art in Washington, DC, hosts exhibition of the works of Cassatt and Degas.

Glossary

art critics—People who are considered experts in art, who judge art, write about it, and help decide how valuable it is.

enroll—To sign up for a class.

formal—Stiff and fancy, not carefree.

mandolin—A small musical instrument with a long neck and strings.

mural—A large painting done directly on a wall.

original—Completely new; never seen before.

pastel—Type of crayon that artists use.

professional—Earning money by doing something, as opposed to just doing it for fun.

rigid—Not able to bend or change.

sketch—A quick drawing that shows a subject's main features.

spontaneous—Happening right at one particular moment without advance planning.

visual arts—Works of art that can be displayed in a room for people to look at, such as drawings, paintings, and sculpture.

Learn More

Books

Alexander, Heather. *A Child's Introduction to Art*: *The World's Greatest Paintings and Sculptures.* New York: Black Dog & Leventhal, 2014.

Cernak, Linda. *Mary Cassatt.* North Mankato, MN: Child's World, 2014.

National Gallery of Art. *An Eye for Art*: *Focusing on Great Artists and Their Work.* Chicago: Chicago Review Press, 2013.

Zaczek, Iain. *Mary Cassatt.* New York: Gareth Stevens, 2014.

Websites

Artcyclopedia: Mary Cassatt
www.artcyclopedia.com/artists/cassatt_mary.html
Provides numerous links to Cassatt paintings that are displayed on the websites of various museums. This site also has links to articles about Cassatt and her work.

The National Gallery of Art
www.nga.gov/collection/gallery/cassatt/cassatt-main1.html
Includes an online "tour" of about twelve of Cassatt's Japanese-influenced prints. On each page, you see one of the works and get information about Cassatt's life.

WebMuseum, Paris
www.ibiblio.org/wm/paint/auth/cassatt
View a selection of Cassatt's paintings, including several of mothers and children. Site also has links to other Impressionist artists.

Index